"ALL MEN CAN SEE THESE TACTICS WHEREBY
I CONQUER, BUT WHAT NONE CAN SEE IS THE
STRATEGY OUT OF WHICH VICTORY IS EVOLVED."

– SUN TZU

THE ART OF WAR

from
SmarterComics™

Sun Tzu

Illustrated by
Shane Clester

Executive Editor
Corey Michael Blake

Creative Director
Nathan Brown

Adapted by
Cullen Bunn and Shane Clester

Summary by
Franco Arda

rtc
A Round Table Companies Production
www.roundtablepress.com

WHILE BASED ON THE ART OF WAR BY SUN TZU, THE ART
OF WAR FROM SMARTERCOMICS™ HAS MAINTAINED THE
IDEAS AND PRINCIPLES FROM THE ORIGINAL TRANSLATION
BUT HAS MODIFIED THEM FOR EASE OF UNDERSTANDING
AND TO CONFORM TO THE COMIC BOOK FORMAT.

INTRODUCTION

Originally inscribed on bamboo strips about 500 B.C., THE ART OF WAR is among the oldest books ever written. It is also one of the most successful books on military strategy ever conceived, and it is still used today by the military, including the U.S. Marine Corps. But its influence has stretched far beyond the military. Sun Tzu's philosophies have been quoted in countless books and movies and taught in business schools. Film makers, athletes, lawyers, negotiators, investors, and even gang members quote from the work.

Don't let the book title fool you—THE ART OF WAR is less about war than about the art of winning. Conflict arises for all of us, whether in business, sports, politics, or personal life. Sun Tzu's goal for THE ART OF WAR was to describe the best way to prevent conflicts in the first place—to outsmart an opponent so that physical battle is not necessary. A general with a reputation for invincibility, Sun Tzu taught strategies for prevailing as quickly as possible against an opponent—with minimal loss of life and property. Every aphorism explained by Sun Tzu (including taking calculated risks and thinking thoroughly before acting) represents a tactic that, when wisely applied, can generate a winning strategy in many areas of daily life.

A warning: this book is deceptive. It is short enough to be read in 30 minutes, but subtle enough to be studied for years—even for a lifetime. Many people have tried to reach into Sun Tzu's book only to find the ancient text too difficult to read. SmarterComics believes this classic should be accessible to a wide audience. That's why we tried something new: modifying the original translation for ease of understanding and to conform to a comic book format. In order to make it most relevant and understandable, we present Sun Tzu's philosophy with illustrated scenes from the 21st century.

It sounds paradoxical, but by better understanding conflict, we might actually prevent conflict and contribute to a more peaceful society.

Your SmarterComics Team

from
SmarterComics™

4

WITH A TEN TO ONE ADVANTAGE, YOUR OVERWHELMING STRENGTH CAN BE DISPLAYED IN SUCH A WAY THAT SURRENDER IS YOUR ENEMY'S ONLY OPTION.

1. IF YOUR FORCES ARE TEN TO THE ENEMY'S ONE, SURROUND HIM.

NOT ONLY WILL THIS APPROACH YIELD THE GREATEST VICTORY— ONE THAT REQUIRES NO BLOODSHED, BUT IT CAN ALSO RESULT IN THE RESPECT, ADMIRATION AND TRUST OF YOUR OPPONENT.

WHEN THE ODDS ARE EVEN, SUN TZU DECLARES THAT BATTLE CAN BE OFFERED. HE DOES NOT RECOMMEND YOU FIGHT.

14

HE WILL WIN WHO KNOWS WHEN TO FIGHT AND WHEN NOT TO FIGHT.

DO YOU THINK WE SHOULD TAKE THIS TO TRIAL?

I FEAR WE MUST. I WILL PREPARE THE DEPOSITION.

CAUTION DOES NOT PREVENT YOU FROM KNOWING WHEN OR WHEN NOT TO WAGE WAR—ARROGANCE DOES.

TO AVOID MAKING DECISIONS BASED ON ARROGANCE, YOU MUST SECLUDE YOURSELF TO A QUIET PLACE AND CONSIDER YOUR SITUATION.

PAINTING A PICTURE IN YOUR MIND OF THE CONSEQUENCES OF YOUR DECISION—BEFORE MAKING THAT DECISION—WILL HELP YOU TO KNOW WHEN YOU CAN FIGHT AND WIN AND WHEN YOU WILL BE UNABLE.

APPEAR WHERE YOU ARE NOT EXPECTED.

CHOOSE YOUR BATTLES CAREFULLY. THE GREATEST ADVANTAGE IS WHEN YOUR OPPONENT DOESN'T KNOW THEY HAVE BEEN SURPRISED AT ALL.

24

FORCE YOUR ENEMY TO REVEAL HIMSELF, SO AS TO FIND OUT HIS VULNERABLE SPOTS.

LET'S GO OVER THIS ONE MORE TIME...

YOU SAY YOU'VE NEVER SEEN THE VICTIM BEFORE... THAT YOU DON'T KNOW ANYTHING ABOUT THE MURDER...

BY USING BAIT AND OBSERVING REACTIONS, A GENERAL CAN COME TO UNDERSTAND HIS OPPONENT'S STRENGTHS AND WEAKNESSES.

YOU KNOW THIS IS PROBABLY GOING TO GO A LOT EASIER ON YOU IF YOU GIVE US SOMETHING TO HELP OUT.

IF YOUR ENEMY REACTS WITH TREMENDOUS FORCE, HE IS MOST LIKELY TO BE POWERFUL.

I ALREADY TOLD YOU, I DON'T KNOW A THING! I WANT MY LAWYER!

34

TO SECURE OURSELVES AGAINST DEFEAT LIES IN OUR OWN HANDS, BUT THE OPPORTUNITY OF DEFEATING THE ENEMY IS PROVIDED BY THE ENEMY HIMSELF.

WHEN OPPORTUNITIES TO DECISIVELY DEFEAT YOUR OPPONENT ARISE, TAKE IMMEDIATE ACTION.

UGH!

CONVERSELY, WHEN YOU BECOME AWARE OF THE IMPOSSIBILITY OF A WINNING OUTCOME, IMMEDIATELY WITHDRAW.

WHILE STRATEGIC DECISIONS REQUIRE DELIBERATE THINKING, TACTICAL DECISIONS MUST BE MADE THROUGH GUT REACTION AND INSTINCT.

IN EVERYTHING WE DO, OPPORTUNITIES MAKE THEMSELVES AVAILABLE QUICKLY AND THEN RETREAT JUST AS QUICKLY.

I'M PUTTING JULIUS IN CHARGE OF GETTING THIS PROJECT FINISHED.

WITH ALL GREAT STRATEGISTS, FROM JULIUS CAESAR TO NAPOLEON, THE VALUE OF TIME—THAT IS, BEING A LITTLE AHEAD OF YOUR OPPONENT—HAS COUNTED FOR MORE THAN EITHER NUMERICAL SUPERIORITY OR THE NICEST CALCULATIONS.

THE TEAM NEEDS ANOTHER COUPLE OF WEEKS TO DISCUSS THE COLOR—

WE'RE GOING WITH THE BLUE.

BY COMBINING SPEED WITH CONCENTRATION (STRIKING WEAKNESS) WE CREATE MOMENTUM.

41

GET THE ADVANTAGE OF THE GROUND

INFORMATION IS PARAMOUNT

REMAIN PATIENT AND FLEXIBLE

THE MARK OF A GREAT GENERAL IS THAT HE FIGHTS ON HIS
OWN TERMS OR HE FIGHTS NOT AT ALL.

About the Author

The legend goes that **Sun Tzu** was born into minor nobility in what is now Shandong, a part of China north of Shanghai. Born "Sun Wu," he was given a good education and wrote a military treatise in order to get noticed and hired by royalty. Sun Tzu expanded his 13-chapter Art of War into 82 chapters and trained the army. Eventually he broke the peace by invading the southern state of Yue. Other conflicts ensued but although his troops were once outnumbered 30,000 to 200,000 he was always victorious. Many successes followed and continued after his death. Some considered his death to be another of his deceptions.

About the Artist

At six years old, Shane Clester realized that most people aren't happy with their jobs. Even as he drew robots just to see if he could, he decided at that young age that he would turn his artistic play into work. As Shane grew older and studied the nuances of art, his initial excitement evolved into fascination. He was compelled by the replication of life through seemingly limited tools, and embarked on a quest to learn technical proficiency. In the early 2000s, Shane studied briefly under Jim Garrison, well-known for his art anatomy and technical skills. Shane then relocated from Arizona to California, where he learned a powerful lesson: You have to study to be an artist, and then you have to learn the business of being an artist.

Shane discovered that he needed to sell himself before he could sell a product. Over the course of the next several years, he broadened his portfolio to include youth-oriented art and comic books, and sourced clients by attending conferences and book fairs. Some of his clients have included leading comic book publisher IDW, Hasbro, Scholastic, Macmillan, and Times of London. Shane is currently a staff artist for Writers of the Round Table Inc. Of his many projects, Shane is particularly proud of *Skate Farm: Volume 2*, a graphic novel he produced, *Mi Barrio*, a comic book adaptation of Robert Renteria's *From the Barrio to the Board Room*, Larry Winget's Wall Street Journal best-selling *Shut Up, Stop Whining & Get a Life* and Chris Anderson's NY Times best-selling *The Long Tail*. He is currently working on Marshall Goldsmith's *What Got You Here Won't Get You There*, and an adaptation of Machiavelli's *The Prince*, both for Round Table Comics.

Art of War QUIZ

Please visit us online on www.smartercomics.com/quiz for the answers.

Q: The very first thing you must do before you go into battle is:

    A. Analyze your enemy.

    B. Count the cost.

    C. Prepare your army.

Q: If you have to go to war, the aim is to:

    A. Win quickly and with minimal loss.

    B. Win quickly at any cost.

    C. Win at any cost.

Q: Going to war without strategy:

    A. Can only be compensated for with smart tactics.

    B. Makes success a mere gamble.

    C. Invokes the best in us.

Q: A weaker army can defeat a stronger army through:

    A. Formlessness

    B. Defense

    C. Offense

Q: A superior number of soldiers does not always equal a greater advantage because:

    A. How you utilize your resources best determines advantage.

    B. How fast you move best determines advantage.

    C. How well you defend best determines advantage.

Q: You can beat a much stronger enemy by:

    A. Focusing your strength against the enemy's weakness.

    B. Focusing your strength against the enemy's strength.

    C. Focusing your weakness against the enemy's weakness.

Q: If you're in battle and you become aware that you cannot win, you should:

    A. Withdraw immediately.

    B. Continue to battle.

    C. Divide your army.

Q: You can beat a more intelligent enemy by:

    A. Sheer force of rapidity.

    B. Prolonging the battle.

    C. Changing your strategy.

Q: If you are unpredictable, you are most likely to:

    A. Fail

    B. Succeed

    C. Retreat

Q: The height of wisdom for a general is to:

    A. Win without a battle.

    B. Win at any price.

    C. Win as quickly as possible.

Look for these other titles from SmarterComics and Writers of the Round Table Press:

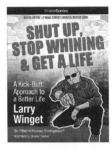

Shut Up, Stop Whining & Get a Life from SmarterComics
by Larry Winget Illustrated by Shane Clester

Internationally renowned success philosopher, business speaker, and humorist, Larry Winget offers advice that flies in the face of conventional self-help. He believes that the motivational speakers and self-help gurus seem to have forgotten that the operative word in self-help is "self." That is what makes this comic so different. *Shut Up, Stop Whining & Get a Life from SmarterComics* forces all responsibility for every aspect of your life right where it belongs—on you. For that reason, this book will make you uncomfortable. Winget won't let you escape to the excuses that we all find so comforting. The only place you are allowed to go to place the blame for everything that has ever happened to you is to the mirror. The last place most of us want to go.

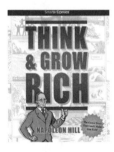

Think and Grow Rich from SmarterComics
by Napoleon Hill Illustrated by Bob Byrne

Think and Grow Rich has sold over 30 million copies and is regarded as the greatest wealth-building guide of all time. Read this comic version and cut to the heart of the message! Written at the advice of millionaire Andrew Carnegie, the book summarizes ideas from over 500 rich and successful people on how to achieve your dreams and get rich doing it. You'll learn money-making secrets - not only what to do but how - laid out in simple steps.

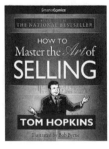

How to Master the Art of Selling from SmarterComics
by Tom Hopkins Illustrated by Bob Byrne

With over one million copies sold in its original version, *How to Master the Art of Selling from SmarterComics* motivates and educates readers to deliver superior sales. After failing during the first six months of his career in sales, Tom Hopkins discovered and applied the very best sales techniques, then earned more than one million dollars in just three years. What turned Tom Hopkins around? The answers are revealed in *How to Master the Art of Selling from SmarterComics*, as Tom explains to readers what the profession of selling is really about and how to succeed beyond their imagination.

Overachievement from SmarterComics
by John Eliot, PH.D. Illustrated by Nathan Lueth

In *Overachievement*, Dr. Eliot offers the rest of us the counterintuitive and unconventional concepts that have been embraced by the Olympic athletes, business moguls, top surgeons, salesmen, financial experts, and rock stars who have turned to him for performance enhancement advice. To really ratchet up your performance, you'll need to change the way you think about becoming exceptional-and that means truly being an exception, abnormal by the standards of most, and loving it. Eliot will teach you that overachieving means thriving under pressure-welcoming it, enjoying it, and making it work to your advantage.

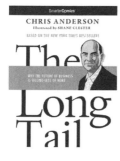

The Long Tail from SmarterComics
by Chris Anderson Illustrated by Shane Clester

The New York Times bestseller that introduced the business world to a future that's already here. Winner of the Gerald Loeb Award for Best Business Book of the Year. In the most important business book since *The Tipping Point*, Chris Anderson shows how the future of commerce and culture isn't in hits, the high-volume head of a traditional demand curve, but in what used to be regarded as misses—the endlessly long tail of that same curve.

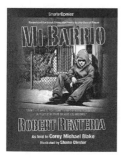

Mi Barrio from SmarterComics
by Robert Renteria as told to Corey Michael Blake
Illustrated by Shane Clester

"Don't let where you came from dictate who you are, but let it be part of who you become." These are the words of successful Latino entrepreneur Robert Renteria who began life as an infant sleeping in a dresser drawer. This poignant and often hard-hitting comic memoir traces Robert's life from a childhood of poverty and abuse in one of the poorest areas of East Los Angeles, to his proud emergence as a business owner and civic leader today.

For more information, please visit www.smartercomics.com

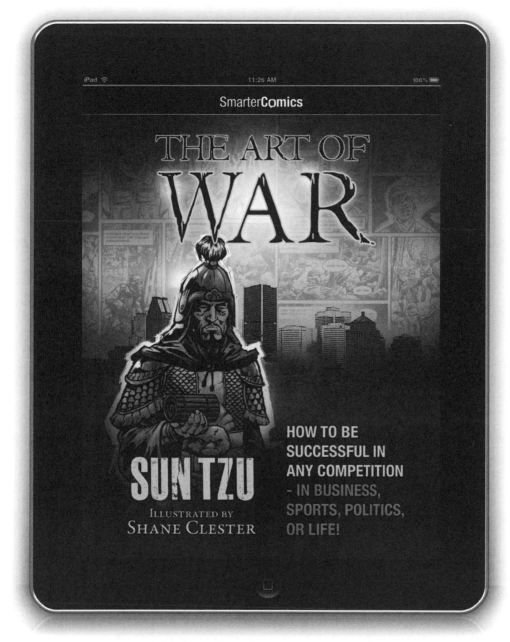

The Art of War and other SmarterComics™ books
are available for download on the iPad and other devices.

www.smartercomics.com

SmarterComics™